DON'T EAT THE QUAIL

… AND OTHER LESSONS LEARNED IN THE WILDERNESS

By Karrie Herzog

Cover illustration by Scott Burroughs (scootertoons.com)

1

TABLE OF CONTENTS

Don't Eat the Quail
"a lesson in contentment"

No Pity Party Allowed
"a lesson in thankfulness"

Beware of the Green-eyed Monster
"a lesson in pride"

Believe it or Not
"a lesson in belief"

Hurry Up and Wait
"a lesson in delay"

It's About Time
"a lesson in perspective"

Happily Ever After
"a lesson in review"

Preface

Ok, I know you are asking yourself, what in the world does "Don't Eat the Quail" mean? Good question... we will get to that in a moment because it's a great story, and I love "story"! I love to read stories, tell stories and watch stories. There is power in story. In fact, I think we are wired to remember and learn from storytelling more than any other kind of communication. How do I conclude such a thing? Well...

Look at Jesus. He knew the power of story. He was, and is, the Master Storyteller. He teaches, encourages, rebukes, warns, motivates and redeems us... all through the power of story.

Look at the Bible... it IS story... it is GOD'S story. We learn about His Character, His Purposes and His Plan through the stories told in the pages of scripture.

Look at our own lives. They are full of stories. Each one comprised of ups and downs, twists and turns; each one different from the other, and yet similar.

Because I am a journaler (is that even a word? oh well, let's just say it is), I have the ability to go back and read much of MY story and let me just tell you, sometimes it ain't pretty. Sure, there are good things: moments when my faith shines and my insights are supernatural. But most of the time, I confess, I am just like the children of Israel who had their share of struggles and setbacks while wandering in the desert.

While reading through the history and accounts of God's people, it is so easy for us to shake our heads and think, "How in the world could they be so blind? They walk through the sea on dry land and the next thing you know they're worshiping a golden calf? That's crazy!

Unbelievable! Inconceivable!" Yeah... you know what's coming don't you? We are just as obtuse. We see and don't believe... we hear and don't understand... we experience and don't remember.

In my own life, I've found that I seem to learn a lesson in faith or trust, only to have to "re-learn" it with each new circumstance! It is very humbling and eye opening to read back over many years of journal entries only to realize that many times I am "learning" the same lessons over and over again. Actually, it reminds me of the whole premise of the movie Groundhog Day where Bill Murray wakes up to the same day, every day, and has a chance to do it over and do it differently. He finds that it is HARD to change and even harder to make those changes stick. Tell me about it.

We read in the Bible that even Paul, one of the most zealous Christians, struggled with this very thing. Here is my paraphrase of his struggle:

"Argh!!!! I'm a mess. The things I want to do, I don't... the things I don't want to do I end up doing... sheesh! Who can help this lost cause? Oh thank you God for Jesus... He can!"

He can, and He does. Jesus really does help us in our weakness and even in our "obtuseness"! When I pick up my journals and look closer, I see that He has been working and is still working in my life. He is making gains. I am learning. I am growing. The process may take longer than I'd like, but it is progress!

Therefore, I invite you, dear reader, to come along with me as I revisit and recount some of the stories and lessons learned (and still being learned) while living in the wilderness. Some might make you laugh… others might make you cry… but hopefully all of them will inspire you to look at your own story and KNOW that He is working all things together for our good!

Introduction

Ok, I know I said I would tell you what "Don't Eat the Quail" means and I will – I promise. But first of all, don't you think I should tell you a little bit about who I am? Aren't you asking yourself, "Who is this chick and why should I read her stories?" Well I would be wondering, so I am going to use this Introduction to literally introduce myself to you.

I think I'd have to describe myself as a motivational speaker and singer who likes to write down my thoughts, feelings, disasters and triumphs in pretty journals. No steno pads for this girl... they must be pleasing to the eye and the cover must call out to me! Over the past two decades, much of the material from my journals has found it's way into messages that I share with women of all ages and stages. I actually have a degree in Women's Ministries which I earned before I ever realized that I had a heart for encouraging women... a God-thing for sure!

In 1990, I had the honor of representing my home state in the Miss America Pageant. Wait... how can it have been that long ago when I am only 30? Strange. Anyway, my official title was Miss Colorado 1990, so I have the honor of always and forever being referred to as a "former Miss Colorado". As a little girl, I had always dreamed of being Miss America... and even though the Top Ten was as close as I would get, the whole experience was truly unforgettable. (Remind me to tell you my swimsuit story someday – God certainly has a sense of humor!)

Following my year of service as Miss Colorado, I had the opportunity to be the resident "fashion expert" on a TV show called Good Afternoon Colorado where I organized and presented on-air fashion shows. Because I happen to love clothes and a good bargain, I had a fantastic time putting together great outfits for a great price. I also learned how to write my own feature stories and even filled in as co-host for the popular afternoon show. I must say, it was a blast and I enjoyed every moment of that season in my life!

And then I got married, had 3 kids, and lived happily ever after... end of story. And if you believe that (you know the saying), then "I've got some swamp land in Florida to sell you." In reality, I went from riding in parades to changing poopy diapers... from motivating audiences to attempting to motivate myself... from wearing a crown to wearing my pajamas all day, every day...

I'm not going to lie - the past 15 years have seemed like a "wilderness" of sorts to me and I've definitely felt like I was wandering around! Don't get me wrong... there have been many wonderful times with my husband, children, family and friends during those years as well. In fact, on paper, were you to look at my life, you'd say I've been pretty blessed and I would have to agree with you. So - why the struggle? Why the pain?

I think I have finally figured out the answer: because I'm human. I know… big revelation, huh? (Hey, stick with me and you'll find little nuggets of wisdom like that all throughout this book!) But seriously, I think there is such encouragement and comfort in knowing that, no matter "who" we are or "what" we've done in our lives, we ALL struggle. True, you don't know me… and I'm pretty sure most of you have never even heard of me. But as you read this book, I'm betting you'll recognize me: I'm your neighbor… I'm your friend… I'm you.

Don't Eat the Quail
"a lesson in contentment"

Welcome to the Wilderness

Ah, the wilderness... if you listen closely you can even hear my heavy sigh as I write those words. According to my online dictionary, the wilderness is "an uninhabited or inhospitable region; a neglected or abandoned area." I must say that I have been living in just such a location for over a decade and I have a love/hate relationship with this place of residence. I can look around and see that I am not alone. As a matter of fact, there are many different kinds of tents pitched in this desert of confinement. For some, the captivity in the wilderness is a physical infirmity or an emotional illness; some may be lost in the desert of a loveless marriage, while others may be struggling with debt or unemployment. The "tent possibilities" are endless, and each of us knows which one we are living in. Personally, my confinement has

16

been of the ministry variety. I can actually look back and trace the beginning of this insatiable longing for a God-sized, God-breathed passion/calling to the year 2000.

Over the years I've asked, begged, and pleaded for God to use me in ways that could only be explained by the miraculous power of God. I happen to be a dreamer, so I wanted "big"... I wanted "grand"... I wanted to change the world for Christ! But instead, God chose to, in the words of author Bob Sorge, put me in a season of "cessation or limitation of ministry" in order to "test the heart motivations". Oh joy. While the reasons for finding ourselves in the desert may vary, there is one thing that all residents have in common: we are waiting.

The Disease of Discontent

When you are waiting in the desert, the temptation is to complain, to be ungrateful, to be impatient and to beg for a change of some kind. Basically, we become discontent. It's a "sickness" of sorts that I refer to as the disease of discontent. It is no respecter of persons, although those with barely enough to survive rarely struggle with discontent... despair maybe, but not discontent. In fact, discontent flourishes in the presence of provision, and its roots settle deep into the fertile soil of disappointment and entitlement. Basically, it saps all joy and purpose from the present moment. How can you tell if you have this disease? Well, I've come up with a "You Know You Are Discontent When" list for your information and diagnosis:

You Know You Are Discontent When...

-Every phrase starts with the words, "I have to..."

-Hours are wasted surfing on the net, not the Ocean

-The more you have, the more you crave

-The grass (say it with me) is greener on the other side

-Your thoughts start with "I wish..." and "If only..."

-No matter what anyone does, it's never good enough.

-No matter what you do, it's never good enough.

-No matter what God does, it's never good enough.

It sure would be great if there were a shot we could take to get rid of this disease of discontent… I'd gladly roll up my sleeve (or even bend over) to find a quick fix for this malady! But alas, a miracle vaccination does not exist, and so we fall into the clutches of discontent where blessings go unrecognized and unappreciated. Unfortunately, one thing leads to another, and the next thing we know, we're eating quail.

Where's the Beef? (I mean Quail)

When the Israelites were living in the wilderness, they needed to eat so God fed them with manna. We are told that this manna was actually "angel's food." I would think, that if it was the food the angels eat in heaven, it must have been be good! Maybe it tasted something like our angel's food cake with cream cheese and butter frosting (with no calories of course). Doesn't that sound heavenly to you? Anyway, every day the children of Israel would wake up and there would miraculously be manna, resting in the dew, ready for them to eat. But after a while, they got tired of eating the same thing day, after day, after day. They wanted something different: they wanted meat! I seriously have to chuckle when I read their story... listen to what they said to Moses:

Numbers 11:4-6

4 And the mixed multitude among them [the rabble who followed Israel from Egypt] began to lust greatly [for familiar and dainty food], and the Israelites wept again and said, Who will give us meat to eat?

5 We remember the fish we ate freely in Egypt and without cost, the cucumbers, melons, leeks, onions, and garlic.

6 But now our soul (our strength) is dried up; there is nothing at all [in the way of food] to be seen but this manna.

Can't you just hear the bitterness in their voices? They kept begging Moses, bugging Moses, and complaining to Moses. Poor guy – He had about had it at this point. He was so "over" all the whining and complaining, that he got angry... and I don't blame him. He said to the Lord (my paraphrase): "I can't take this anymore! Why do I have to be responsible for these people? I am not their Dad. I shouldn't have to carry them around like babies. All they do is beg and complain. Just kill me now."

I feel his pain. When my kids were little, the constant whining almost drove me nuts! And guess what? God doesn't like whining either... so when Moses came before God to whine about the Israelites whining... He had heard enough. God basically said, "Okay... I'll get you some help and you tell the people to get ready. If it's meat they want, it's meat they're gonna get." (Of course, you have to imagine God saying that with a sarcastic tone, because that's how I hear it in my head)

As the story goes, God "answered" their cries and sent them meat to eat. He used the wind to make quails drop out of the sky and into their camps... more quail than they could even eat. They probably thought, "Finally, we have meat!" So what did they do? They gorged themselves on the quail... horded the quail... and they got sick. Some of them even died. Not good.

I'll have the Manna please

Now here's how my story and the children of Israel's story correlate. Not too long ago I was tired of being in the wilderness. Imagine that. I was discouraged... I was

22

weary… and I kept complaining, whining, and begging God saying, "Please, please, please send me something to do! I'm going crazy without some purpose or calling. I'll take anything… just send me something!" Almost immediately the phone rings, and it's a mom whose children go to school with my children. She proceeds to tell me about an online resource she and her husband were creating for Jr. High kids that would help them to learn and grow in their relationship with Jesus. One of the things they were producing was a series on friendship, and, she said as she was driving along, my name just "popped" into her head to read for the part of the mother in one of the videos. I immediately thought to myself, "Well, this must be it! This must be what I prayed for because I just got done asking and she called. I'm not doing anything else, so why would I say no?" So, I said yes. And then as the day went on I thought, "I don't want to do this. I'm not an actor. I don't even like to act. I'm going to have to learn lines and go to all the rehearsals…" I was dreading it before it even began. And yet, I went back and forth, back and forth, thinking, "Maybe I shouldn't do it... But I want to do SOMETHING... But if I do it, I won't enjoy it... But didn't I just pray and this dropped into my lap? That has to be a sign, right?"

Of course, it might have helped if I had prayed about it first and not jumped to conclusions. I should have reminded myself of what I say all the time: "Just because you can, doesn't mean you should!" So, I contacted the mom and told her the truth. I apologized and explained that acting just wasn't my "thing". She completely understood and assured me that it would all work out. And then, as I hung up the phone, I had an "Aha" moment - I realized with a start, "Oh my goodness... I didn't eat the quail! I passed the test!" I had said yes, not because I wanted to, not because God was telling me to, and not because I was the right person for the part. I had said yes, because I was discontent with where God had me. News flash Karrie… wrong reason! If I had gone to that audition, I would have ended up eating quail and getting "sick". I might have even died a little (spiritually speaking that is).

Hook Me Up

Looking back, I have to ask, "What led me to the point of almost eating quail?" I've since realized that the underlying problem was not that I wanted meat per se, I am somewhat of a vegetarian, but it was actually a lack of contentment in my heart that put me in that precarious position. In her book *Simple Abundance,* the author Sarah Ban Breathnach says, "What is missing from many of our days is a true sense that we are enjoying the lives we are living." Discontent finds a way to seep into our lives, coloring our view and twisting our perspective. This is precisely what our enemy wants to happen. Satan's strategy is to steal, kill, and destroy and when dissatisfaction and longing for a different life pervades our thinking, he can literally do just that: steal, kill, and destroy our todays. When that happens, Satan wins and we lose.

How then, can I change from living a life that is hindered by discontent, to living a life that is full of contentment? Is it merely a matter of being a positive thinker? Does one only need to slow down and make a list of the things we should be thankful for? While those things certainly couldn't hurt, Paul says that the secret to being content is found in Christ. In Philippians 4, verses 11 and 12, he says that contentment has nothing to do with circumstance, and everything to do with Jesus. In fact, Paul insists that it will take nothing less than a supernatural infusion of Christ's strength in us.

In other words, I need to be hooked up to a "J.C. IV" line that is delivering a constant flow of supernatural strength into my bloodstream. Because, contrary to popular belief, it is not a matter of changing our self-talk or slapping ourselves upside the head saying, "Get a grip woman!" (Although I have been known to do such a thing) The remedy is supernatural, and, as Paul also points out, it is learned. In order to learn something, I have to study it... practice it... and actually do it! And what better place to learn such a skill than in the wilderness?

So, my fellow desert dwellers, here is the deal... or as I like to borrow from the cartoon Kim Possible, "Here's the sitch." When we are in the wilderness, and it seems like nothing is happening, and we are tempted to breed discontent, remember: God... is... working. We are changing. We are learning to listen, to grow, and to be content in this desert. Yes, it is hard... and we daily face the temptation to complain about the food. But here is the cool part – here is what we have, that the children of Israel didn't have: their story. And if we are smart, we won't condemn them, but instead, we'll read their story and learn. We'll LEARN, my friend. We'll learn to hook up our IV line, thank God for the manna, and heed the voice in the wilderness that says, "Don't Eat the Quail!"

No Pity Party Allowed
"a lesson in thankfulness"

Let's Get This Party Started

I want to share with you a little well-known secret about me… I love parties. Not all parties mind you, just costume parties and pity parties. At one shindig, I get to dress like someone else… at the other, I wish I were someone else. One soiree is perfectly harmless, and the other is undoubtedly destructive. While many friends like to join me for the dress up bash, no one seems to want an invitation to the sympathy gala. Surprise, surprise…

It's Party Time

Back in the "good ol' days", my husband and I used to love the TV show Alias. We ended up watching it one night by accident and from that moment on, we were hooked... and we weren't the only ones. Every Sunday night, there would be a group of about 10-15 people who would come over to watch Alias with us on our "big screen". Let me just tell you, we took our viewing policies very serious. Yes, we had policies. For instance, in the event that we might miss something important, absolutely no talking was allowed when the show was on and offenders were relegated to the basement to watch on the small screen. Ah, what we would have done for a DVR back then!

For those of you who did not have the privilege of watching this iconic show, Jennifer Garner played the part of Sydney Bristow: an international spy recruited out of college and trained for espionage and self-defense. In my opinion, one of the best parts of the show was all the disguises and costumes she got to wear while completing her missions. Tell me, who wouldn't want to be a sassy blue-haired punk rocker one

31

moment, and an elegant Russian debutante dripping in diamonds the next? Sign me up!

The temptation to dress up ourselves proved too hard to resist, so every season, for both the premiere and the finale, Chet and I would have an Alias costume party. We even mailed out Top Secret invitations for added effect. Everyone, and I'm talking everyone, would go all out and come in elaborate costumes, crazy make-up and various wigs. However, one year, without telling any of us, several of the men decided to come as the "good guys" and ambushed the house from the back yard. They burst through the doors, dressed in suits with red laser guns yelling, "EVERYONE, GET DOWN... ON THE FLOOR, NOW!" Man, did we have fun! Whenever my girls, who were very little back then, hear me tell all the Alias party stories, they say it's not fair – they want to dress up and pretend to be spies too. Well, I do have all 5 seasons on DVD...

It's My Party and I'll Cry If I Want To

As much fun as I had hosting our Alias parties, I must admit that over the years, I have ended up hosting many more of another kind of party: the pity party. One of my favorite books of all time (and movies of all time) is Pride & Prejudice. I love the romance, the portrayal of culture, and the way Jane Austin points out, none too subtly I might add, many of our human foibles. Speaking of foibles, Mrs. Bennet, the main character's mother, happens to be quite a trip. She is always whining... always complaining... and always feeling sorry for herself. Whenever I watch the movie I think, "Sheesh woman, pull it together! What is your problem? I'm glad I'm not like that... surely I'm nothing like her... right?" Wrong. As I look back over the span of time I've been living in the wilderness, I am embarrassed to concede that I have displayed a "Mrs. Bennet" spirit on more than one occasion. It's an attitude that says (with the back of the hand on the forehead), "Nobody can tell what I suffer! But it is always so. Those who do not complain are never pitied." Funny, but true... at least it is in my life.

When I'm honest with myself, I find that I want to be pitied. I want all my hard work and sacrifice to be acknowledged... how else will anyone appreciate "what I suffer" if I don't complain about it? Ouch. I delude myself into thinking that all of my moaning and groaning will get me the attention I "deserve." However, when I choose to focus only on myself, I end up in a perpetual state of entitlement... and that's not helping anything or anyone. Look what happened to the children of Israel when they focused on themselves and their circumstances:

Numbers 21:4-5

4 And they journeyed from Mount Hor by the way to the Red Sea, to go around the land of Edom, and the people became impatient (depressed, much discouraged), because [of the trials] of the way.

5 And the people spoke against God and against Moses, Why have you brought us out of Egypt to die in the wilderness? For there is no bread, neither is there any water, and we loathe this light (contemptible, unsubstantial) manna.

Wow... they sound so petulant and ungrateful don't they? But before we go pointing our finger, we might want to take a little gander at our own attitudes and the words that come out of our mouths. I know I can easily fall into the trap of disdain and end up not appreciating the life God has given me. No doubt about it... something has to change, and that something would be me.

A Bug's Life

In the movie *A Bug's Life*, there is a praying mantis named Manny who happens to be a professional circus performer. In one scene, as he is masterfully delivering his lines, he is hit square in the face with a tomato. Responding indignantly to the slight, he yells, "Ingrate!" Of course my children have no idea what that word means, but I do. There have been many times, as I've read back over numerous journal entries filled with ungratefulness, that I've wanted to throw a tomato at myself and shout, "Ingrate!" It's embarrassing! Why can't I seem to fight the temptation to have a "poor me" attitude? Why do I keep giving in to self-pity when I am so blessed?

One of our pastors said in a sermon recently, that self-pity is actually an emotional drug. Yikes. That set me back for a moment. He wasn't talking about the kind of drug that is helpful. I think he was referring to the kind of drug that is "an illicit substance that causes addiction, habituation, or a marked change in consciousness". Is this hitting you like it hit me? Self-pity is actually a drug... and for believers, it's an illegal one. If God's Word says we are to be thankful all the time, which it does, then we are most certainly committing a "crime" when we partake of the narcotic. Paul says in 1 Thessalonians 5:18 that we are to "Thank [God] in everything [no matter what the circumstances may be, be thankful and give thanks], for this is the will of God for you [who are] in Christ Jesus [the Revealer and Mediator of that will]." I hate to break it to you, but the truth is, we cannot be high on the drug of self-pity and thank God at the same time. It's impossible.

I'm Checking Myself In

So where does that leave me? I can't speak for you, but I know if I'm going to beat this thing, I need help. Looks like it's time for some self-pity rehab. In college, when we wanted to sleep in on Sunday, we would joke that we were going to Bedside Baptist with Reverend Sheets. Well, I'm not joking when I say I need to check myself in to Jehovah Rapha Rehab with Doctor Divinity. Seriously, if I am going to rid myself of a habit-forming drug like self-pity, I am going to need full-time assistance and some supernatural meds... and I know just where to find them.

Proverbs 4:20-22

20 My son, attend to my words; consent and submit to my sayings.

21 Let them not depart from your sight; keep them in the center of your heart.

22 For they are life to those who find them, healing and health to all their flesh.

The medicine we need, the cure for our addiction to self-pity, is not only found IN the Word of God, it IS the Word of God. When we read the Word, speak the Word, memorize the Word, sing the Word etc., we experience health and healing. Soon our thoughts will turn toward the One whose *"divine power has granted to us all things that pertain to life and godliness, through the knowledge of him who called us to His own glory and excellence - 2 Peter 1:3*

When we fill our minds and our mouths with God's Word, our attitudes will change from thankless to thankful. An awareness of the many blessings in our lives will flood our souls. And instead of focusing on the ways we wish our lives were different, we will look at our days and see them as gifts… seeing the ordinary as extraordinary. We will be healed. We will be changed. We will be free. Sounds good to me. Let's link arms, gird our loins, and do this thing together. Let's relinquish our sense of entitlement and be brave enough to get the help we need. Not only will our lives be so much fuller, but I have a sneaking suspicion that the lives of those around us will be too.

Beware of the Green-eyed Monster
"a lesson in pride"

O, beware, my lord, of jealousy;

It is the green-ey'd monster,

which doth mockthe meat it feeds on.

(William Shakespeare, *Othello*)

Envy slays itself by its own arrows

If jealousy is the green-ey'd monster, then it has an evil twin - and it's name is envy. Both thrive in the harsh conditions of the desert and can sneak up on their "prey" un-detected. One might even mistake them for the same animal and yet, they are very different. Joseph Epstein makes the distinction in his book simply titled, *Envy.* "Most people, failing to pick up the useful distinction, mistakenly use the two words interchangeably. The real distinction is that one is jealous of what one has, envious of what other people have. A self-poisoning of the mind, envy is usually less about what one lacks than about what other people have." Unlike jealousy, envy is considered to be one of the "Seven Deadly Sins", joined by wrath, greed, sloth, pride, lust, and gluttony. In other words, it's not good. Once again, Epstein's words seem to say it best: "Little is good about envy, except shaking it off, which, as any of us who have felt it deeply knows, is not so easily done."

Why Not Me?

Numbers is the book of the Bible that recounts in detail, the span of time that the children of Israel spent wandering in the wilderness. There are 36 chapters in this book, and right about in the middle, comes a little chapter with only sixteen verses... sixteen very important verses.

Numbers 12

1 NOW MIRIAM and Aaron talked against Moses [their brother] because of his Cushite wife, for he had married a Cushite woman.

2 And they said, Has the Lord indeed spoken only by Moses? Has He not spoken also by us? And the Lord heard it.

3 Now the man Moses was very meek (gentle, kind, and humble) or above all the men on the face of the earth.

4 Suddenly the Lord said to Moses, Aaron, and Miriam, Come out, you three, to the Tent of Meeting. And the three of them came out.

5 The Lord came down in a pillar of cloud, and stood at the Tent door and called Aaron and Miriam, and they came forward.

6 And He said, Hear now My words: If there is a prophet among you, I the Lord make Myself known to him in a vision and speak to him in a dream.

7 But not so with My servant Moses; he is entrusted and faithful in all My house.

8 With him I speak mouth to mouth [directly], clearly and not in dark speeches; and he beholds the form of the Lord. Why then were you not afraid to speak against My servant Moses?

9 And the anger of the Lord was kindled against them, and He departed.

10 And when the cloud departed from over the Tent, behold, Miriam was leprous, as white as snow. And Aaron looked at Miriam, and behold, she was leprous!

11 And Aaron said to Moses, Oh, my lord, I plead with you, lay not the sin upon us in which we have done foolishly and in which we have sinned.

12 Let her not be as one dead, already half decomposed when he comes out of his mother's womb.

13 And Moses cried to the Lord, saying, Heal her now, O God, I beseech You!

14 And the Lord said to Moses, If her father had but spit in her face, should she not be ashamed for seven days? Let her be shut up outside the camp for seven days, and after that let her be brought in again.

15 So Miriam was shut up without the camp for seven days, and the people did not journey on until Miriam was brought in again.

First of all, can I just say, that it seems a little bit unfair that both Miriam and Aaron were talking against their brother and yet she was the only one "punished"? Miriam: leprosy... Aaron: nothing. Of course, I'm not privy to all the facts here. Maybe she was the one to start it all, or, perhaps the envy ran deeper in her veins... I doubt we will ever know the truth. Regardless, the object lesson is clear: envy makes God angry.

I find it interesting that this chapter follows the quail story in the book of Numbers. The Israelites had just experienced God's wrath for complaining about the manna so I would think that Miriam and Aaron would have been a little more cautious with their thoughts of dissent. However, I'm guessing that the resentment and disapproval they felt for their brother had been building up for some time and could remain hidden no longer. This passage does not say if their talking against Moses was in a private conversation or if it was in the midst of a crowd. Nevertheless, the Lord heard every word, and He was not pleased.

Family Meeting

When the kids were little, my husband instituted what would become known in our household as the "Family Meeting." Periodically, he would call all three children into the living room where the meeting always took place. First, he would have them line up on the couch, and then he would remind them to refrain from talking and to hold all questions until he was done. Sometimes, the subject matter of the meeting was to tell them of an upcoming activity or surprise… those times were fun. However, there were also occasions when the Family Meeting was a time for discipline and instruction… and those times… not so fun.

When God heard that Miriam and Aaron were dissing their brother, their "meek, gentle, kind and humble" brother, God called a Family Meeting. He basically said something like this: "Look, Moses is my guy – He is faithful – I trust him - I choose to talk with him like no other – I even allow him to see Me - So why would you even dare to insult him?" Yikes! That's not what you want to hear. I wonder how Moses must have felt when he realized his siblings had been talking about him behind his back? The situation was just bad all around.

As the cloud of God's presence left them, it was clear that His judgment would remain: Miriam was as white as snow. What a shock! I think if I were her, I would have started to scream and cry and, for all we know, maybe she did. The author of Numbers does not share those kinds of details with us. We do read, however, that when Aaron looked at her and realized what had happened, he did something very commendable that I want to point out. He immediately said to Moses, "Oh my lord, I plead with you, lay not the sin upon us in which we have done foolishly and in which we have sinned." Aaron used the words "us" and "we". He could have easily considered himself lucky to escape God's wrath and just kept his mouth shut... but he didn't. Could that heart attitude, which God knew was residing inside of Aaron, actually have been the reason he escaped the retribution of leprosy? I don't know... God does look at the heart... something to think about for sure.

Not only did Aaron respond to Miriam with mercy and love, Moses did as well. He could have been angry with her, justifiably so one might argue, and let her "pay" for her sin. Instead, he displayed the very character that made him stand apart from all the men on the face of the earth: he cried out to God and begged Him to heal her right then and there. While God did not choose to take her leprosy away immediately, He did take into consideration the plea of Moses. In the end, Miriam only had to suffer the disease temporarily while living outside the camp for seven days. All I can say is that I am so very, very, thankful that God does not still put leprosy on those who experience the sin of envy today. For if He did, I fear that I too might have found myself "white as snow" (and I'm not talking about the fairytale here)!

What About Me?

It all started at church. You know... I could just stop right there and let you fill in the blanks because I really don't want to be transparent and honest right now. I mean, who would be crazy enough to admit to harboring one of the Seven Deadly Sins? Apparently, (hand half raised), that would be me. As much as I would like for you to have a spotless opinion of me, I find that I am being compelled by my Heavenly Father to tell the truth, ugly as it may be. So here we go.

It all started at church. Actually, it all started at an event for the church. Well, I suppose it started at a meeting, for an event, for the church. Honestly, I guess it really started in my heart, at a meeting, for an event, for the church. (I'm starting to sound like the song *There's a Hole in the Bottom of the Sea* – *"There's a flea on the wing on the fly on the frog on the bump on the log in the hole in the bottom of the sea."* But I digress… let's start back at the beginning of this story.

As you well know by now, at this point in my life, I was a desert dweller who wanted to be a Canaan colonist. I was longing for, looking for, and begging for, my "Promised Land". I wanted God to use me in a mighty way - whatever that even means. I just wanted out of the wilderness and I was weary of God's apparent silence on the matter. I felt overlooked, unwanted and insecure…

The month was June and the event was "ENCOUNTER 2010: A 3-night experience designed to create a space and environment where people can encounter breakthrough and transformation through the outpouring of the love of Jesus Christ." Oh I had an "encounter" all right, but it was more like *Close Encounters of the Third Kind...* more on that later. A vision casting team was assembled to plan all of the event details and my best friend Chrysti and I were both included. The team asked us if we would be willing to take charge of the music for the 3-night event, and we were greatly honored. Up to this point, we had been co-leading worship at church about once a month, on Wednesday nights, so this was a great opportunity to do more.

Chrysti and I went through copious amounts of music trying to put together the right songs for each night (we needed about 30 songs = 10 per night). After many hours of planning, the set lists were decided; musicians were secured; practice CDs were burned; and rehearsal times were scheduled. And that's when it all started to fall apart... for me. When it was time for the band to get together for our first rehearsal, something became apparent to me very quickly: you can't have two leaders. Well duh, you might be saying, but you have to understand that up until that point,

Chrysti and I had co-led worship many times without any incident.

However, with such a large amount of music to not only be learned, but also to be led, there needed to be only one leader - it was just too confusing otherwise. Being that Chrysti is my BFF, I knew her deepest heart's desire was to lead worship with a talented worship band, so, I told her that I thought she should be the one to take the reigns for Encounter. She was very hesitant at first, but I assured her that it was the right thing for everyone involved. Oh how I wish the story ended there... unfortunately it does not.

Look Out She's Gonna Blow!

As Encounter drew nearer and rehearsals continued, I should have stopped and realized that *"Something wicked this way comes."* But instead, I allowed the seeds of resentment and competition began to grow unchecked in soil that was ripe with discouragement and self-doubt. And before I knew it, those seeds had grown into full-blown envy. Practices were torture... I would sit there, feeling sorry for myself, and keep an invisible account of the numerous ways I would have done things differently - all the while applauding "yours truly" for being unselfish enough to let Chrysti lead by herself. I told you this was ugly. No one knew, of course, that this was festering inside of me. I hid it well... for a while.

The first two nights of Encounter, I did a pretty good job with keeping a lid on my feelings. Or so I thought. As it became more and more obvious to everyone that Chrysti was truly operating in her God-given talents and gifts, it became more and more obvious to me that I was in trouble. As this horrid "thing" began to rise up in me, wanting to rear it's ugly head, I kept shoving it back down. I felt like an Alien had invaded my body. Every time someone would come up and compliment Chrysti, or tell her how gifted and anointed she was, I could feel the monster growing. I actually fought with myself saying, "What is your problem Karrie? You know that leading worship is Chrysti's desire and passion – not yours! Why are you struggling with this? Get a hold of yourself!"

Now, you have to know, that it's not as if there weren't people who were speaking encouraging things to me during that time as well... because there were. But did I let those words heal and mend my wounded soul? Oh no. I continued to give in to jealousy's evil twin, which, according to that insightful little book *Envy,* "blocks out clarity, both about oneself and the people one envies, and it ends by giving one a poor opinion of oneself. Envy clouds thought, clobbers generosity, precludes any hope of serenity, and ends in shriveling the heart." Yep... that about sums it up.

By the third and final night, I just wanted it all to be over with so I could go back to the happy-go-lucky relationship I had with my best friend and pretend all of this never happened. God, however, had other plans. About two thirds of the way through, as we were singing songs of praise to the King, God "let" me see and feel the true condition of my heart and I was so overcome with grief and shame, that I couldn't even continue for one more moment. I had to go to the back, put down my microphone, and walk off the stage... in the middle of the song. I felt like Isaiah who, when in the presence of God and His Holiness, could only fall on his face and reply, *"Woe is me! For I am undone and ruined, because I am a man of unclean lips...." (Isaiah 6:5)*

After leaving the stage, I went into the green room and fell apart. How could I have let it come to this, I wondered? And how in the world was I going to pull myself together enough to be able to go back out there and sing? I still had a song I needed to lead, for pete's sake! In that moment, as I sobbed and confessed my unworthiness, guess what happened? God met me with grace. As I earnestly repented and asked for His forgiveness, He met me with mercy. Amazing. And yet, isn't that the Gospel in all its beauty - our Father choosing to give us what we don't deserve, while at the same time, electing not to give us what we do deserve? I think that calls for a hearty AMEN!

Thankfully, I did not become leprous, on the outside anyway, and I headed back out to finish the night. Afterwards, many of our friends came over to our house to eat and to celebrate all of the amazing things God had done in the life of our church and in the hearts of those who came to Encounter. As the night drew to a close, one of my dear friends decided to stay and wait until everyone else had left... and then she lovingly "cornered" me. She could tell that I wasn't quite myself, and I could tell she wasn't going to leave until I fessed up. Being that she was a trustworthy friend, I went ahead and shared a little bit about what had been going on inside of me.

She asked questions... I cried... and then we even laughed together when I picked up the Bible and ended up reading in James that we are to *"Consider it wholly joyful, my brethren, whenever you are enveloped in or **encounter** trials of any sort or fall into various temptations."* I couldn't believe it... the verse said "encounter"! My friend then strongly encouraged me to be honest with Chrysti and tell her everything, or else it would, in her estimation, end up coming between us. Nah, I thought... it's really unnecessary to bring it all up now... it's over... it's done... it's all good. Uh huh. That was Friday night... but Sunday mornin was a'comin!

Confession is Good for the Soul

It all started at church. Wait, where have I heard that before?
Anyway, it was Sunday morning, Encounter had ended two
days before, and I thought I was out of the woods. Chrysti
and I had just dropped off our children in their respective
classes, and we were headed over to "big church". Then, lo
and behold, a mutual friend happened to stop us to talk about
Encounter. She expressed to both of us how much she had
enjoyed all of the music, and then she turned to Chrysti and
said, "But you... YOU were amazing!" I'm not sure what
else she said, because I couldn't stand there and listen to
anymore so I took off. Some best friend, huh?

A couple of minutes later, as I was walking briskly toward
the Family Worship Center, I   heard Chrysti running up
behind me saying, "Wait up... wait up." I know, I know...
go ahead... you can say it: "Aw, poor Chrysti." She asked

me if there was anything wrong and I replied, with total honesty, "Nope. Nothings wrong." I'm sure no one would be surprised to know that Chrysti was well aware that there was, indeed, something very wrong. Nevertheless, she continued to treat me with the patience and loving-kindness I did not deserve. I think I'll keep her.

Somehow, we made it through the service and then I hightailed it out of there during the last song. I could tell Chrysti was crying and, while I would like to think it was because of the convicting words of the Pastor, I knew it was because of the hurtful wounds of her friend. I must say, that as I walked away, I literally despised myself. Never, had I been more convinced of the depravity of my human nature, than in that very moment. I cried and cried and fought God all the way home. I didn't want to talk to Chrysti about it... I didn't want to be honest... I didn't want to admit that I was filled with resentment and envy.... And yet I knew, deep

down inside, I was at a crossroads of sorts. I had a choice…
and that choice would affect one of the most precious
friendships I've ever experienced. I could either stuff the
beast of envy back down inside, hoping that, eventually, it
would go away on it's own – or, I could call Chrysti and get
rid of it for good.

Love Conquers All

Right then and there, I decided not to waste one more minute
as a slave to the sin of envy. I called Chrysti and divulged
everything… the good, the bad and the ugly (it was mostly
bad and ugly). I think that confession was one of the hardest
things I have ever had to do in my life and yet, at the same
time, it was somehow one of the most rewarding. I asked for
her forgiveness, which, she immediately extended lovingly
and graciously. Of course, there were many, many tears shed,

but there were also many moments of laughter and supernatural revelation.

Chrysti helped me recognize that the envy I was feeling wasn't rooted in a desire to take away the opportunities she had to use her gifts and talents... nor was it fueled by a longing to do the same thing she was doing. She also reminded me of all the wonderful things that were spoken over me during the three days of Encounter and reiterated what she knew to be my true passions and longings. Boy did I need that encouragement! I guess that's what friends are for. Great... now all I can hear is Dionne Warwick singing, *"Keep smilin', keep shinin', knowin' you can always count on me, for sure, that's what friends are for...for good times and bad times, I'll be on your side forever more, that's what friends are for....".* Sorry, now you're going be singing that song all day long. At any rate, as Chrysti and I continued to process through all the muck and yuck, the Holy Spirit gently

63

revealed to me that my struggle with envy was a direct result of a couple of things. Only a "couple" of things, you ask? Ok, only a couple of MAJOR things. First of all, I was, somewhat unknowingly, nursing a deep, deep feeling of disappointment that God's plan for my life at that moment was to be in a season of confinement or imprisonment. Bob Sorge, in one of the best books I have ever read, *The Fire of Delayed Answers*, says this: "One of the most painful dynamics of the prison season is the feeling of being excluded from everything God is doing around you. You sit and watch others progressing in God, rejoicing in the Lord, moving about with great freedom and fruitfulness. And here you sit." I couldn't have said it any better.

I had allowed this season, this time when God was intentionally pulling me back, to disquiet and discourage me. Instead, I needed to realize that God designed this season of struggle so that He could not only prune and cut off that which was dead, but also so that He could spend time with me and prepare me for what was to come. God needed to work on my character - big time - and James says that when we encounter trials and tribulations, we also experience growth.

James 1:2-4

2 Consider it wholly joyful, my brethren, whenever you are enveloped in or encounter trials of any sort or fall into various temptations.

3 Be assured and understand that the trial and proving of your faith bring out endurance and steadfastness and patience.

4 But let endurance and steadfastness and patience have full play and do a thorough work, so that you may be [people] perfectly and fully developed [with no defects], lacking in nothing.

If I will only choose to let the qualities that God is trying to cultivate in me have full play, then I will also have the wonderful promise of becoming what James refers to as a person who is fully developed with no defects. Yay! Just knowing that something good would come from all of my strife was great news. However, before I got too excited, God reminded me that the pruning wasn't over yet. There was still one more "major" issue He needed to deal with.

Pride Goes Before a Fall

After showing me that it was the depth of my disappointment that had given breath to my envious heart, the Holy Spirit then revealed to me that the real source, the lifeblood if you will, of this offensive sin, is pride. Oh dear. I guess you could even say that envy is merely the result of wounded pride. Pride says, "I deserve better than this." - "Why is she getting all the attention?" - "I have a lot to offer and no one appreciates me."

Pride is, quite simply, an overestimation of one's own competence or capabilities and it is utterly detestable to a Holy God. Was not pride possibly the first sin ever committed? I'm not talking about Adam and Eve or even their sons Cain and Abel. I'm referring to the god of this age, the ruler of this present darkness, and the father of lies: Satan. He was once a highly exalted angel, living in the matchless presence of God... and it wasn't good enough. He wanted more... felt like He deserved more... and declared that he would have more. That arrogant attitude was Satan's pride in action, and it led to his downfall – literally.

Isaiah 14:12-15

12 How have you fallen from heaven, O light-bringer and daystar, son of the morning! How you have been cut down to the ground, you who weakened and laid low the nations. [O blasphemous, satanic king of Babylon!]

13 And you said in your heart, I will ascend to heaven; I will exalt my throne above the stars of God; I will sit upon the mount of assembly in the uttermost north.

14 I will ascend above the heights of the clouds; I will make myself like the Most High.

15 Yet you shall be brought down to Sheol (Hades), to the innermost recesses of the pit (the region of the dead).

I will, I will, I will, I will, I will... five times Satan disregarded God's authority and said, "I will." "But I would never go that far, you say... I would never suppose myself to be equal to or exalt myself above God." And yet, every time we grumble and complain, haven't we done just that? When we think our lives should be different, and spend our time fighting the season we find ourselves in, are we not assuming that we know more than God by thinking we have a better plan? I'm afraid the answer is yes. Pride is ugly my friend, and it must be dealt with if we are ever to be truly free of envy and it's consequences.

Come Out, Come Out, Wherever You Are

Looking back now, I realize that God loved me too much to let my sin remain hidden. He wanted to expose what was lurking just below the surface and He did the same thing with His chosen people. God intentionally let the Israelites wander in the desert in order to humble them and test them… to know what was in their minds and hearts.

I had no idea I was capable of the kind of deep-rooted envy that would permeate my soul… and with my best friend as the recipient no less! I wonder if Miriam was also shocked at her capacity for envying the very brother she had so lovingly saved from death as an infant. I don't know the answer to

69

that, but I do think envy caught both me, and Miriam, by surprise.   So don't be unaware my friend.   Whenever you spot the green- ey'd monster lurking in the shadows of your heart, be assured that his evil twin is not far behind and run… run like the wind!

Believe it or Not
"a lesson in belief"

You Snooze, You Lose

Every year my children's school designates special days when all of the kids get to dress up according to a certain theme. I think it's designed to be fun for the kids and agony for the parents. Tell me, how in the world do you dress up a kid for "All Creatures Great and Small Day"? One year, I completely forgot about "Bible Character Day", so I grabbed a piece of fabric, cut a hole in the top, threw it over my little guy's head, tied it with some string and said, "There you go... you look just like... uh... Moses." Due to the fact that I am so highly organized, ahem, I have been known to be out the night before a dress up day, frantically searching for something that will at least give the appearance that I am efficient and creative. Somehow, our children's costumes, or lack thereof, seem to be a Rorschach test of sorts, detecting possible underlying disorders in our psyche. All I have to say is, I like crazy hair day and pajama day… I've got those down pat.

It's Western Day

Several years ago, when my oldest daughter Brooke was about 10 years old, she and I had a little "altercation" regarding a particular dress up day: Western Day. Surprisingly, I was feeling pretty good about myself because I had actually remembered to write it down on the calendar. I had even gone out ahead of time and bought things for the kids to wear. However, when I informed Brooke the night before that the next day was going to be Western day, she didn't believe me. I told her I was telling the truth, and yet she still didn't think I knew what I was talking about. She said it was hard for her to believe me because no one, including her teacher, had said anything about it. So I took her over to the calendar and showed her where I had written in bold words, **"Western Day"**, and assumed the debate was over. The next morning, she came downstairs with another shirt underneath her western one so that, just in case it wasn't Western day, she would have something to wear. I kind of took it personal and got upset with her. I asked her, "Why would I lie to you?" To further prove my case, I went and found the Monday letter for her class and showed her where it clearly stated that it was going to be Western Day that day. She started to cry and apologize, saying that she was sorry that she doubted me... not one of my prouder parenting moments.

As I shut the door on her retreating form, grumbling about her lack of belief in me, I immediately heard God say to me, "Uh huh... that is exactly what you do to me. I give you my Word, full of promises, and you don't believe me. Why would I lie to you? Why don't you believe me?" Why indeed.

I Kid You Not

I've noticed that many times, before Jesus would even try to teach His disciples about a concept or promise, He would start by saying, "I assure you, most solemnly I tell you...." If He were speaking those words in this day and age it would go something like this: "Look, I am dead serious here – I am not lying – I am telling you the truth...." Why in the world would Jesus, the Son of God, have to emphasize the fact, over and over, that He was not messing around? Because we are a people plagued with doubt. The way I see it, doubt was the sin that the little devil on Eve's shoulder, or rather the serpent in her garden, used to tempt her when he said, "Did God really say, 'You must not eat from any tree in the garden'?" - "You will not certainly die," the serpent said to the woman. "For God knows that when you eat from it your eyes will be opened, and you will be like God, knowing good and evil." Boom! Doubt made its debut and it has been headlining ever since.

When in Doubt, Throw it Out

In my opinion, doubt is a dangerous and slippery slope, because, left unchecked, it can quickly morph into unbelief. While they may be related, there is still a big difference between the two. Kurt von Schleicher at Fish For Souls says, "Doubt is a matter of the mind. Unbelief is a matter of the heart. Doubt is when we cannot really understand what God is doing and why He is doing it. Unbelief is when we refuse to believe what God's Word says and we subsequently fail to do what He tells us to do. Unbelief is disobedience and it leads to more of the same. We mustn't confuse the two."

The book of Hebrews reveals that it was, in fact, the sin of unbelief that evoked God's anger against the children of Israel; resulting in forty years of wilderness wandering, and a whole generation failing to enter the Promised Land.

Hebrews 3:12-19

12 [Therefore beware] brethren, take care, lest there be in any one of you a wicked, unbelieving heart [which refuses to cleave to, trust in, and rely on Him], leading you to turn away and desert or stand aloof from the living God.

13 But instead warn (admonish, urge, and encourage) one another every day, as long as it is called Today, that none of you may be hardened [into settled rebellion] by the deceitfulness of sin [by the fraudulence, the stratagem, the trickery which the delusive glamor of his sin may play on him].

14 For we have become fellows with Christ (the Messiah) and share in all He has for us, if only we hold our first newborn confidence and original assured expectation [in virtue of which we are believers] firm and unshaken to the end.

15 Then while it is [still] called Today, if you would hear His voice and when you hear it, do not harden your hearts as in the rebellion [in the desert, when the people provoked and irritated and embittered God against them].

16 For who were they who heard and yet were rebellious and provoked [Him]? Was it not all those who came out of Egypt led by Moses?

17 And with whom was He irritated and provoked and grieved for forty years? Was it not with those who sinned, whose dismembered bodies were strewn and left in the desert?

18 And to whom did He swear that they should not enter His rest, but to those who disobeyed [who had not listened to His word and who refused to be compliant or be persuaded]?

19 So we see that they were not able to enter [into His rest], because of their unwillingness to adhere to and trust in and rely on God [unbelief had shut them out].

Walk By Faith, Not By Sight

I don't know about you, but I don't even want to entertain thoughts of doubt or unbelief. I don't want to wander for forty years or completely miss out on the Promised Land God has for me. So... what do I do? I cultivate the exact opposite of doubt and unbelief: faith. Faith is perhaps the single most important component of our walk as believers, for we read in Hebrews that without faith, it is impossible to please Him. That verse always floors me. Without faith... (the assurance, the confirmation, the title deed of the things we hope for, the proof of things we do not see and the conviction of their reality – the faith that perceives as real fact what is not yet revealed to the senses)... without that kind of faith, we cannot please Him - it is literally impossible.

It breaks my heart to think of all the times I have operated out of a sinful heart of unbelief instead of a heart overflowing with faith. God sent His own Son to die for me, for cryin out loud… what more does He have to do to convince me that He is Who He says He is, and will do what He says He will do? My faith falters most, I think, when God's ways don't "line up" with what I understand His word to say. Obviously, the problem is not with God – the issue is my limited understanding. Proverbs 3:5-6 says that I need to *"Lean on, trust in, and be confident in the Lord with all your heart and mind and do not rely on your own insight or understanding. In all your ways know, recognize, and acknowledge Him, and He will direct and make straight and plain your paths."* That verse makes it pretty clear that my insight or understanding cannot be trusted, or, as I often say, "I'm skewed".

Therefore, I have got to stop trying to figure things out! I must resist the temptation to constantly draw conclusions. I find that I invariably want to wrap everything up in a nice, neat little bow and unfortunately, that's not a very realistic expectation. In that case, I guess I must conclude that things will not always make sense to me.

Believing is Seeing

Pastor Blake, one of the pastors at our church, said in a sermon that, "God doesn't owe us answers... we are to walk by faith, not by answers." My problem is that I wait for my experiences to catch up with my faith before I fully believe that what He says is true. Nevertheless, God is not asking me to believe in an outcome, He is asking me to believe in Him: the One who is trustworthy... the One who is faithworthy (Yeah, I know I just made up that word, but I like it)! Just look at these verses that speak of God's character:

2 Samuel 7:28

28 O Sovereign LORD, you are God! Your words are trustworthy, and you have promised these good things to your servant.

Psalm 9:10

10 Those who know your name will trust in you, for you, LORD, have never forsaken those who seek you.

Psalm 111:7

7 The works of his hands are faithful and just; all his precepts are trustworthy.

Deuteronomy 7:9

9 Know, recognize, and understand therefore that the Lord your God, He is God, the faithful God, Who keeps covenant and steadfast love and mercy with those who love Him and keep His commandments, to a thousand generations,

Numbers 23:19

19 God is not a man, that He should tell or act a lie, neither the son of man, that He should feel repentance or compunction [for what He has promised]. Has He said and shall He not do it? Or has He spoken and shall He not make it good?

The scriptures are full of such descriptions and the list could go on and on… When you think about it, the whole Bible is, in effect, God's personal character witness. And in my estimation, the bottom line is this: God is Who He says He is and will do what He says He will do. Not only can I believe Him, I MUST believe Him if I desire to please Him. I can't allow myself to get hung up on my minimal understanding or on the ways and means God chooses to carry out His word. I

83

can either choose to believe what circumstances seem to attest – or - I can believe that my loving Heavenly Father is telling me the truth when He hands me a cowboy hat and says, "It's Western Day"!

Hurry Up and Wait
"a lesson in delay"

The Waiting Game

When you are in the wilderness, there is a LOT of waiting, and I hate to wait. I don't like waiting in lines. I don't like waiting in traffic. I don't like waiting, period. In fact, waiting goes against my human nature. You know what I'm talking about... it's that nasty nature that God wants to change... yeah, that one. Lately, I have felt like a woman who is 9 months pregnant and past her due date who is trying everything she can to make the baby come out: she's walking, she's running, she's eating spicy foods etc. If I could figure out a way to break my water, believe me, I would.

You know, I probably drive God crazy. I drive my own self crazy! Over the past decade, in my quest for purpose and passion, I've come up with 10 different book proposals, 5 different businesses, a plethora of merchandising ideas and tried to make a 100 different doors open... all to no avail. Why? God wanted me to wait. Did you know that God actually ordains times of waiting and delay? I would even go as far as to say that waiting is God's M.O. - His "modus operandi". In other words, it's how He likes to work. Rats.

It's School Time

My husband Chet is an avid hunter who likes to have everything he needs to be successful and so, of course, we have a hunting dog. His name is BB (as in BB gun) and he is a German shorthair who I am told is quite talented. I haven't braved the cold weather yet to watch him in his element, but I'll take my husband's unbiased word for it. BB's exceptional ability to point and wait and then retrieve is not all instinct, however. O no, we (and when I say we, I mean

Chet) sent him to school… hunting school. He trained with an expert for over a month and when he came back, he was one lean, mean, hunting machine! He knew what to do, when to do it, and most importantly, how to listen to commands. The other day Chet wanted to show me just how well trained BB is so he called me outside and said, "Watch this."

It was time for dinner and BB loves, and I mean LOVES, his food. If he is hungry and we aren't feeding him quickly enough, he will actually have a hissy fit. He will kick his metal bowl and stand at the door and bark. Then he'll go over and kick it again and bark until we get him some food. Wait a minute, who has who trained here? I know, I know. Anyway, as I was saying, it was eatin time and Chet was in front of BB's bowl and he was prancing all around and getting excited (BB that is, not Chet). My husband dumped the food in the bowl, right under BB's nose and said, "Wait for it... wait for it." I watched poor BB as he whined and wiggled and squirmed. He would look at the bowl and then look at Chet, look at the bowl, then look at Chet. Drool was literally dripping out of his mouth and he waited... and waited... and waited.... After what seemed like forever, Chet finally said, "Ok." Man, did that dog gulp down his food! I was so proud of him and I praised him for what a good dog he was - as if he even cared! He was probably thinking, "Whatever lady, just get out of my space, I'm eatin!"

Later that night, as I was writing in my journal about my aversion to waiting, I started laughing. I thought to myself, "I'm just like BB! I feel like God has placed a dream, right under my nose, and He is saying, "Wait for it... wait for it...." And there I am, whining, and wiggling, and squirming, with drool dripping out of my mouth, just waiting to hear Him say, "Ok." Nice visual, huh?

At first glance, this "teaching method" might seem cruel or unnecessary. Why make us wait? Is God just being mean? Is He toying with us? The answer is "No"... he is not mean and he is not toying with us. He loves us more than we can imagine and that love wants what is best for us. And so, He waits.

Everything is Not What it Seems

As I think about God and His penchant to wait, I am reminded of the resurrection of Lazarus. It is such a great story - you've got to read it with me:

John 11:1-6, 14-17

1 Now a certain man named Lazarus was ill. He was of Bethany, the village where Mary and her sister Martha lived.

2 This Mary was the one who anointed the Lord with perfume and wiped His feet with her hair. It was her brother Lazarus who was [now] sick.

3 So the sisters sent to Him, saying, Lord, he whom You love [so well] is sick.

4 When Jesus received the message, He said, This sickness is not to end in death; but [on the contrary] it is to honor God and to promote His glory, that the Son of God may be glorified through (by) it.

5 Now Jesus loved Martha and her sister and Lazarus. [They were His dear friends, and He held them in loving esteem.]

6 Therefore [even] when He heard that Lazarus was sick, He still stayed two days longer in the same place where He was.

14 So then Jesus told them plainly, Lazarus is dead,

15 And for your sake I am glad that I was not there; it will help you to believe (to trust and rely on Me). However, let us go to him.

16 Then Thomas, who was called the Twin, said to his fellow disciples, Let us go too, that we may die [be killed] along with Him.

17 So when Jesus arrived, He found that he [Lazarus] had already been in the tomb four days.

Can you believe it? At first, it's hard to understand why Jesus would intentionally stay away until his friend had been dead for four days - but I want you to read verse six again. Do you see the word "Therefore"? Jesus loved Martha, Mary and Lazarus and therefore He... what? Ran right to them? Sent word that He was on His way? Immediately commanded Lazarus to be healed? No... He waited. He waited because He loved them! One would think He'd have rushed to the scene. But Jesus knew better - He knew what the waiting would accomplish and He tells His disciples that He was glad He wasn't there when Lazarus died. What? He was glad? Yes... He was glad because He knew it would help the disciples to believe, to trust, and to rely more on Him. Jesus was setting the scene for a miracle resurrection – Now that's worth the wait!

Throughout scripture we see that God likes to wait until all hope is seemingly lost; until the body's been dead for 4 days; until the fire is hot; until the lions are hungry; until the womb is 90; until the enemy is a giant. Seems backwards doesn't it? Yet I have learned during this wilderness season, that waiting has intent and design. I think the only thing worse than having to wait would be if waiting had no purpose. Sometimes we get a glimpse of those purposes while we wait and sometimes they become clear in hindsight. Although I would venture to guess that there are many purposes that we will only fully understand once we are with Him in glory. Even then, the fact remains that waiting has meaning, and for those of us who have been in the wilderness for a while, that is good news!

Eat Humble Pie... It's Good!

While He certainly could have kept them in the dark, God didn't make the children of Israel wait until heaven to find out what He had been doing in the forty years they wandered and waited in the wilderness. In the eighth chapter of Deuteronomy God graciously reveals His purposes:

Deuteronomy 8:1-16

1 All the commandments which I command you this day you shall be watchful to do, that you may live and multiply and go in and possess the land which the Lord swore to give to your fathers.

2 And you shall [earnestly] remember all the way which the Lord your God led you these forty years in the wilderness, to humble you and to prove you, to know what was in your [mind and] heart, whether you would keep His commandments or not.

3 And He humbled you and allowed you to hunger and fed you with manna, which you did not know nor did your fathers know, that He might make you recognize and personally know that man does not live by bread only, but man lives by every word that proceeds out of the mouth of the Lord.

4 Your clothing did not become old upon you nor did your feet swell these forty years.

5 Know also in your [minds and] hearts that, as a man disciplines and instructs his son, so the Lord your God disciplines and instructs you.

6 So you shall keep the commandments of the Lord your God, to walk in His ways and [reverently] fear Him.

7 For the Lord your God is bringing you into a good land, a land of brooks of water, of fountains and springs, flowing forth in valleys and hills;

8 A land of wheat and barley, and vines and fig trees and pomegranates, a land of olive trees and honey;

9 A land in which you shall eat food without shortage and lack nothing in it; a land whose stones are iron and out of whose hills you can dig copper.

10 When you have eaten and are full, then you shall bless the Lord your God for all the good land which He has given you.

11 Beware that you do not forget the Lord your God by not keeping His commandments, His precepts, and His statutes which I command you today,

12 Lest when you have eaten and are full, and have built goodly houses and live in them,

13 And when your herds and flocks multiply and your silver and gold is multiplied and all you have is multiplied,

14 Then your [minds and] hearts be lifted up and you forget the Lord your God, Who brought you out of the land of Egypt, out of the house of bondage,

15 Who led you through the great and terrible wilderness, with its fiery serpents and scorpions and thirsty ground where there was no water, but Who brought you forth water

out of the flinty rock,

16 Who fed you in the wilderness with manna, which your

fathers did not know, that He might humble you and test you,

to do you good in the end.

God flat out reveals to His people that He ordained the wilderness years to humble them, to test them, and to see what was in their hearts. He wanted to see if they would follow His commandments and He wanted them to be in position where they could personally experience His provision. He also let them wander around in order to discipline them and instruct them. Ultimately though, He says that everything He did was so that he could do GOOD to them in the end and bring them into the promised land! That's a pretty good purpose don't you think? So, if that was God's design for the Israelites, and He is the same yesterday, today and tomorrow, then couldn't I conclude that His purpose in my season of wilderness is the same? I think I can!

I need to be reminded, constantly it seems, that this season is for my good. Unfortunately, I can't pass up the stuff that comes before the Promised Land. There's the humbling, the proving, the testing, the hunger, the discipline and the instruction. I just want to skip to the "good" part. Nevertheless, God wants to put us in situations and circumstances that will reveal our hearts, both to us and to Him. He desires to reduce and rid us of our independence, pride, exultation, arrogance and self- sufficiency. Believe it or not, that too is a "good" thing. Really… it is. We don't want any of that nasty stuff hanging around when we're living in the Promised Land.

Expectant, not Expecting

A friend of mine once said, "The longer the soil goes barren, the deeper the nutrients grow and it will be richer and produce more fruit crops." Fortunately, when there is a season of waiting... a delay between the promise and the possession... our "soil" is becoming richer. Character is formed, trust is built, and faith is increased. But only if, and that's a big if, we will learn to value the time waiting in the wilderness. That is easier said than done. Look how quickly our fickle hearts can turn:

Psalm 106:12-13

12 Then [Israel] believed His words [trusting in, relying on them]; they sang His praise.

13 But they hastily forgot His works; they did not [earnestly] wait for His plans [to develop] regarding them.

Let's face it...we forget. We fail to remain in a state of readiness where we trust in his timing, plan and provision. We want to run ahead of God and "help" Him get moving! One day, when I was sharing with Chet that I was struggling with all of the waiting and doing nothing, he said that I was like the "2 chicks", Mary and Martha, who had Jesus over for dinner. One was too busy doing things while the other sat at the feet of Jesus - waiting and listening to him. He said I was doing the right thing by waiting and not rushing around doing a bunch of things... good words... good husband.

Waiting is not easy... and most of the time it's not very fun. I find that I must daily ask myself: am I willing to wait or will I resist the work He is trying to accomplish? Will I trust that He loves me and has a purpose in this season, or will I give in to doubt and unbelief? Will I patiently "wait for His plans to develop regarding me", or will I forge on ahead without Him? I will be honest with you... some days I don't want to wait. Some days I grow weary and want to take matters into my own hands. And yet, thankfully, most days, I find that I do want to grow and mature and become the woman God wants me to be... I do want to make right choices. You know what that means, don't you? I have to stop trying to go into labor. No more talk of an early delivery or breaking my water... I must now be expectant, not expecting... I must be willing to wait.

It's About Time
"a lesson in perspective"

Timing is Everything

Have you ever noticed that God is all about timing? Not surprisingly, the first story we read in Genesis is in no way nebulous. "In the beginning..." is followed by a very detailed account of the timing involved in Creation. The passage does not say, "When God felt like it, He created the heavens and the earth. And then, sometime later, He made the birds of the air and the beasts of the field...." No, the story is very specific because God's timing is specific. All you have to do is peruse the Bible to see that God is very particular about the order of things: 7 days here, 3 days there, 40 days here, 40 years there. He has a plan and that plan includes a very precise timeline. Nowhere do we see this more evident than in the birth of Jesus. Paul recounts it this way:

Galatians 4:4-5

4 But when the right time finally came, God sent his own Son. He came as the son of a human mother and lived under the Jewish Law,
5 to redeem those who were under the Law, so that we might become God's children.

Not only was the nativity of Jesus meticulously planned, but the span of His life and ministry were also carried out to the letter according to God's design. We don't know much about Jesus' life as a child, and we'll never know for sure at what age He was fully aware of His Father's plan. Be that as it may, we do know that by age of 12 Jesus had a pretty good idea what was up.

A Mother's Nightmare

Those of you who have ever had a child missing, for any length of time, know the feeling of sheer panic that overtakes you when a child is lost. I have endured that paralyzing fear on 2 occasions. The first time was when my youngest, Brady, was about 3 or 4 years old. We had spent the weekend up at our church camp and as we got ready to leave we couldn't find him anywhere. (Of course the camp was in the mountains with a lake and a raging river near by!) I am so grateful that everyone dropped what they were doing and began to search, because all I could do was fall to the ground and cry out to God. After what seemed like hours, which in reality was probably only about 20 minutes, they found him down by the river with a couple of our fellow campers. I can't even begin to explain the relief that flooded my soul in that moment.

The second time was a couple of years ago and involved my middle child Kendra who was 9 at the time. Some very good friends of mine offered to bless my children and take all three of them to see the movie Monsters vs Aliens. They were so excited to see the movie and I was so excited for some alone time! It wasn't very long after they left however, that I got a call from my friend telling me that they were at the theater buying snacks and couldn't find Kendra... she had gone to the restroom and then vanished.

I must admit, I didn't handle this disappearance any better than I did the first one with Brady. I fell to the floor and began praying and crying and even screaming. Everyone there was searching for her... the theater workers... the on-site security... and no one had seen her. Our good friends lived about 2 minutes from the theater, so her husband jumped in his car to go help. Chet quickly jumped in his truck to go look, and just as he was about to arrive, my friend called to tell me they had found her. Apparently, there were two theaters showing the same movie and when she left the restroom she accidentally walked into the wrong movie theater! Let me just tell you, I hope I NEVER have to go through that again!

You may recall, that Mary had a similar experience with Jesus when he was only 12 years old. The family had just attended the Passover Feast in Jerusalem and, assuming that Jesus was somewhere in the caravan, they set out for home.

The Family Business

Luke 2:41-52

41 Now His parents went to Jerusalem every year to the Passover Feast.

42 And when He was twelve years [old], they went up, as was their custom.

43 And when the Feast was ended, as they were returning, the boy Jesus remained behind in Jerusalem. Now His parents did not know this,

44 But, supposing Him to be in the caravan, they traveled on a day's journey; and [then] they sought Him [diligently, looking up and down for Him] among their kinsfolk and acquaintances.

45 And when they failed to find Him, they went back to Jerusalem, looking for Him [up and down] all the way.

46 After three days they found Him [came upon Him] in the [court of the] temple, sitting among the teachers, listening to them and asking them questions.

47 And all who heard Him were astonished and overwhelmed with bewildered wonder at His intelligence and understanding and His replies.

48 And when they [Joseph and Mary] saw Him, they were amazed; and His mother said to Him, Child, why have You treated us like this? Here Your father and I have been anxiously looking for You [distressed and tormented].

49 And He said to them, How is it that you had to look for Me? Did you not see and know that it is necessary [as a duty] for Me to be in My Father's house and [occupied] about My Father's business?

50 But they did not comprehend what He was saying to them.

51 And He went down with them and came to Nazareth and was [habitually] obedient to them; and his mother kept and closely and persistently guarded all these things in her heart.

52 And Jesus increased in wisdom (in broad and full understanding) and in stature and years, and in favor with God and man.

I love that the Bible is full of people we can relate to. I appreciate this passage for the glimpse that I get into the heart of Mary, knowing that she too was susceptible to panic. Can you imagine? I barely made it 30 minutes and Jesus was missing for days! But as I look closer, I realize this story is less about Jesus being lost and more about God's perfect timing in the life of His Son.

It's All Going According to My Plan

When I read through this story, I thought it was intriguing that Mary and Joseph found Jesus after searching for three days. Not one, not two, but three days. My spiritual radar went up when I saw that little detail so I decided to look up the significance of the number 3 in scripture and I was blown away! I can't even begin to tell you what I found - it is crazy… crazy cool. (You'll have to Google it for yourself sometime) Basically, the number three represents something being "specially complete" and is used to signify God's purpose or His will. The number is also meant to grab your attention and point to the event that follows. I think that's the case in this story. God wanted to shine a spotlight on His

Son... He wanted to reveal that Jesus was not your average, everyday 12 year old.

When his parents finally find him in the temple, they are at a loss as to why Jesus would do such a thing. And it is here, in His response, that we discover this fact: Jesus knew exactly who He was, and what He was sent here to do. His calling was to be in His Father's house and to do His Father's business. Which makes what follows even more significant in my opinion: He went back with his parents, was "habitually obedient" to them, and grew in wisdom, stature and favor... for 18 years. He had to wait for 18 years, people! Just envision with me how hard it must have been for Jesus. He must have been chomping at the bit!

I used to wonder, "Why in the world would God wait until Jesus was 30 years old? Just think what He could have accomplished from the age of 20 to 30! That's a whole decade where Jesus could have been healing people, speaking God's Word and bringing heaven to earth." As expected, there was a very good reason for the delay: timing. I am sure there were countless things that needed to line up perfectly before Jesus could step into His 3 year ministry (there's the number 3 again)! I just discovered that one of those reasons was, that according to Jewish tradition, a rabbi could not speak publicly and with authority until they were age 30. Did you know that? I didn't know that. I do now. And do you want to know what this little piece of information says to me? "Karrie, honey, you don't have a clue."

His Ways Are Not Our Ways

One of my spiritual mentors, Pastor Blake Mattocks, says that, "The promises of God belong to us... but His ways and means do not." Repeatedly throughout scripture, we read that God's ways are not our ways and His thoughts are not our thoughts. Isaiah says it this way:

Isaiah 55:8-11

8 The LORD says, "My thoughts are not like yours. Your ways are not like mine.

9 Just as the heavens are higher than the earth, so my ways are higher than your ways, and my thoughts are higher than your thoughts.

10 "Rain and snow fall from the sky and don't return until they have watered the ground. Then the ground causes the plants to sprout and grow, and they produce seeds for the farmer and food for people to eat.

11 In the same way, my words leave my mouth, and they don't come back without results. My words make the things happen that I want to happen. They succeed in doing what I send them to do.

Paul exclaims the same truth in Romans 11:33 when he declares, *"Oh, the depth of the riches and wisdom and knowledge of God! How unfathomable (inscrutable, unsearchable) are His judgments (His decisions)! And how untraceable (mysterious, undiscoverable) are His ways (His methods, His paths)!"*

I find it amusing that I can read those verses and still think I can figure out what God is doing in my life. Sure, there are times when He will give me an insight or show me something in hindsight but for the most part, in the words of a popular catch phrase, I must "Let go and let God." I can just hear my best friend say, "Good luck with that."

Is it Time Yet?

For me, waiting in the wilderness has been very frustrating because it seems like such a waste of time. In fact, I frequently remind God that I'm not getting any younger and I keep begging Him to move me out of this desert. I must sound just like my children who have little to no patience. I can't even breathe a word to them about any fun activity ahead of time, or else they will incessantly bug me and stand by the front door asking, "Is it time yet? Is it time yet?" I'm guessing God uses similar parenting skills with me. If He told me about a "fun activity" ahead of time, I too would be standing by the front door asking, "Is it time yet? Is it time yet?"

The fact of the matter is that God's timing is perfect. He is never late. He is never early. He knows what He is doing and He has a plan. David agrees when he declares, *"My times are in Your hands....*" I think one of the most quoted and beloved verses in the Bible is *Jeremiah 29:11 - "I know the plans I have in mind for you, declares the LORD; they are plans for peace, not disaster, to give you a future filled with hope."* Notice what God does NOT say... He does not say, "I know the plans I have for you; they are plans to frustrate you, disappoint you and give you less than you had hoped for." Even though the verse may not say those words, I think that sometimes, I believe in my heart that it does. Oh me of little faith.

I have found, that the only way to counter my wayward and faithless heart, is to constantly remind myself that God loves me and that His timing has meaning and purpose. Case in point: Jesus. Not only did Jesus need to wait to start His ministry because of Jewish tradition, but He also needed to wait for another reason: it would take time to grow in favor with God and man.

115

I have a great friend, Jeff Rasor, who, as he has watched me struggle during this wilderness season in my life, has been so faithful to ask me how I'm doing and how he can pray for me. The other day he sent me a message and said that God had given him a "word" for me. Let me just tell you, I was eager to hear what he had to say! (When you have been sojourning in the hot desert for a long time, a Word from God is like a cool fresh drink of water) Here is what Jeff shared with me: "Favor and fruit are two entirely different things. Favor actually transcends fruit. There can be favor on someone even when you don't see obvious fruit or activity. God's favor is on us in the seasons of waiting so that there will be fruit later." Huh.

As I meditated on those words, I realized I had been assuming that fruit was an indicator of favor. However, when you look at the lives of people in the Bible, many of them went through a time when it seemed favor was absent. For example, Joseph spent a long time in prison... Daniel was cast into a lion's den... and David had to hide in caves for years.... Was God's favor on them during those "barren" years? Absolutely. Did crazy abundant fruit result from those times? Sure did. The same was true for the Messiah. During the 18 years that Jesus was doing carpentry instead of public ministry, He was growing in favor with God and man.

You wouldn't think Jesus would have to grow in favor with God... with man, yes... but with God? I would have assumed He had 100% of God's favor from the get go. But no – it would appear that Jesus needed to grow in favor with man AND God during the years he waited. That way, once the timing was right, He could burst on the scene full of power, knowledge and fruit! Hallelujah! That's good news! That means God's favor is also on me in this wilderness season, and, at the right time, I too will step into my ministry and bear fruit.

Hindsight is 20/20

Much of my spiritual growth flourished under the teaching of an amazing man named Dr. Rick Ferguson. For over a decade, my husband and I had the privilege of learning, laughing, and living alongside this beloved mentor/friend. I will never understand why God chose to take him home at age 47. But, what makes no sense to us, makes perfect sense to an all-knowing, all-loving Father. One of the things Pastor Rick used to say, that I will always remember is, "If we knew what God knew, we would want what He wants."

Such words of wisdom... and yet the conflict remains. For in our limited understanding, we find that we do not know what He knows and therefore struggle to want what He wants.

There have been many, many, times I have cried out to God in desperation saying, "God, please, please, please… You have got to help me! I know, that if I knew what You knew, then I'd want what You want. But the fact is, I don't know what You know, so I am having a really hard time wanting what You want!"

Over the years, we have been blessed to have many different people come and go through our Sunday night Bible studies, and one such person was a young man who would join us whenever his busy college schedule would allow. One night, he shared a story with us about how, as a little boy, he was obsessed with all of the latest and greatest toys on the market. He told us that when he would see the toy commercials on TV, or when they would be out shopping somewhere, he would ask his mom if she would buy him some toys and her answer would be "No."

Then, he would go over to his friends' houses where, of course, they had all the toys that he wanted! He would end up coming home and begging his mom to let him have what his friends were so "lucky" to have. There were times, he said, that his mother would go ahead and get him one of those toys. But, to his dismay, most of the time she said no. He admitted that as a young kid, he was pretty mad at his mother... he just couldn't understand why she would say no and deny him such small requests.

Sometime later, when he was much older, our friend decided it was time to buy his dream car. He searched and searched, and finally found the perfect one... only to be let down. The hard reality was, that even after saving for years, he didn't have enough money to buy the car. (Now would be a good time to grab a tissue... I'm just sayin.) One day, after seeing how disappointed he was that he wouldn't be able to afford his dream car after all, his mother walked up to him and handed him a check.

Knowing that this day would come, his mother had been writing down the approximate price of every little toy that her son had wanted so badly during his childhood. I'm sure you know by now what's coming next. When she totaled up the cost of all those toys, the amount was exactly what he needed to buy his car. To say that he was blown away, is an understatement. He finally understood why his mother chose to say no to all the "little" things that he had wanted: she had a much greater purpose and plan in mind for her son.

That story is such a beautiful picture of the wisdom, love and restraint that our Heavenly Father employs in the lives of His children. He knows that sometimes, what we ask for is, in the long run, not the best thing for us. And then again, sometimes His answer is yes to our requests... either way, we must learn to trust in His infallible timing.

No Time Like the Present

Each of our lives has it's own story to tell. Some of you may be in a wilderness season right now like me. Some of you may have just come out of one or, unbeknown to you, are headed into one. And yet, no matter where we are in our journey, my hope is that all of us will come to believe that God does have a good plan with a perfect timeline. Solomon, who is considered to be one of the wisest men ever to live, came to a similar conclusion.

Ecclesiastes 3:1, 11-14

1 There is a right time for everything, and everything on earth will happen at the right time.

11 God gave us the ability to think about his world, but we can never completely understand everything he does. And yet, he does everything at just the right time.

12 I learned that the best thing for people to do is to be happy and enjoy themselves as long as they live.

13 God wants everyone to eat, drink, and enjoy their work. These are gifts from God.

14 I learned that anything God does will continue forever. People cannot add anything to the work of God, and they cannot take anything away from it. God did this so that people would respect him.

Years ago I actually wrote a song about God's timing based on Solomon's words in Ecclesiastes. As you read the lyrics, let this sure promise encourage you: our times truly are in His hands.

There is A Time

A hand to hold

A smile to share

A bond to mold

A love to care

A tear that falls

A laugh that rings

A voice that calls

A heart that sings

There is a time for everything

For every man, Pauper or King

Ours is to live and see what life brings,

For, there is a time for everything.

A stone to throw

A wound to feel

A faith to grow

A hope to heal

A soul that's meek

A spell that's long

A trust that's weak

A will that strong

There is a time for everything,

For every man, Pauper or King

Ours is to live and see what life brings,

For, there is a time for everything.

Happily Ever After
"a lesson in review"

So here's the part where I tell you that the waiting, the wondering, and the wandering, has been worth it all. This is when I reveal that God has finally said to me the same thing he said to the Israelites at the end of their forty year journey: "You have dwelt long enough at this mountain." But guess what? He hasn't said that to me yet. I'm actually still in the wilderness.

Yes... you read that right. I am still waiting for God to show me what he has planned for the next season in my life. I must admit, that if it were up to me, I would never have chosen to wait this long. Who would? Who would choose waiting over receiving, suffering over blessing, or character over comfort? Not me. In fact, I would have done things very differently and would have gladly shared my blueprints with God if He had just asked. Shockingly, despite my willingness to help, God did not ask my opinion on the matter… imagine that!

Tis' the Season

Whenever I look at my experiences, or hear others talk about their journeys, I find this truth to be glaringly evident: our lives are made up of many different seasons. Some seasons are fruitful… some seasons are barren… and some seasons are, quite honestly, absolutely wretched. We must remember though, that seasons change. Uh oh… I feel another song coming on – sing it with me – *"To Everything, Turn, Turn, Turn… There is a season, Turn, Turn, Turn… And a time to every purpose, under Heaven. (louder now!) A time of love a time of hate… A time of…."* So sorry… I got a little carried away there… just ignore me and keep reading.

127

The point I am trying to make is this: for those of us who are still in the wilderness, there is good reason to take heart. Why? Because, despite how it seems to us right now, God will not leave us here. We do eventually get to leave this place. Our dilemma is that we just don't know when, where, or how. The reality is, that as long as we are here on this earth, there will be times of both wilderness living and Promised Land living. Unfortunately, or should I say fortunately, we don't get to choose the timing of either one. God is the one who decides and decrees the days and times of our lives.

David declares this truth when he writes in the Psalms, *"I will cry to God most high, to God who accomplishes all things for me. On the day I called, Thou did answer me. The Lord will accomplish what concerns me; Thy lovingkindness, O Lord, is everlasting; do not forsake the works of Thy hands. Thou didst form my inward parts; Thou didst weave me in my mother's womb. And in Thy book they were all written, the days that were ordained for me, when as yet there was none of them."*

I have no idea how much more time I have left in this wilderness season, but here is what I do know: I'm on the donkey, and I'm moving out of the desert... albeit slowly at times... but I am moving. Right now, my responsibility is to love God and serve Him with what He has put right in front of me - not looking forward or backward. I must purpose in my heart to remember everything He has taught me during this time, and consequently, choose to trust Him implicitly. For when I am able to actually let go; to believe he will accomplish what concerns me; to have no blueprints of my own; then, and only then, will I find that my heart and mind will be flooded with a peace that passes all understanding. And that right there, my friends, is wilderness living at it's best.

A word about the Author

Karrie Herzog has been motivating and encouraging audiences with both her words and her voice for the past 21 years. She has a Bachelor of Science degree in Women's Ministries and, while in college, traveled extensively throughout the United States, Canada and even Korea with the Sounds of Heritage singing group. In 1990, Karrie had the honor and privilege of being crowned Miss Colorado, going on to place in the Top Ten at Miss America, as well as winning one of the 6 coveted preliminary awards.

After her busy year as Miss Colorado, she joined the show Good Afternoon Colorado on 9KUSA, Denver's local NBC affiliate, as the resident "fashion expert". Karrie not only organized on-air fashion shows, but also learned how to write her own feature stories and even filled in as co-host for the popular afternoon show. She continues to use her talents in media by providing voice over for various projects.

Loving all things creative, Karrie has been involved in many things, including owning her own handmade card business. Many of her designs were even featured in retail venues such as Nordstrom's and Macy's, as well as card stores around the world. Her love for music has been expressed in many ways over the years, and for over a decade, she was the featured vocalist for a big band group called The Joe Peterson Orchestra.

Currently, Karrie is a Professional Home Economist (stay at home Mom), with three wonderful children. She is somewhat of a vegetarian who happened to marry an avid hunter - go figure! Karrie continues to do motivational speaking and singing, and in her free time, she enjoys reading, reading, and... more reading! If she had more energy, she might even enjoy something like ballroom dancing or pilates. Oh well, maybe someday.

www.ingramcontent.com/pod-product-compliance
Lightning Source LLC
LaVergne TN
LVHW021512080426
835509LV00018B/2490